Remedies of Poetry

TRACY CONNOLLY

Published 2023 by Your Book Angel
Copyright © Tracy Connolly

The characters are all mine, any similarities with other fictional or real persons/places are coincidental.

Printed in the United States
Edited by Keidi Keating
Layout by Rochelle Mensidor

ISBN: 979-8-9876155-7-7

Acknowledgement

I will start by thanking my fiancé, Padraig who is my critique and strongest pillar of support.

My daughter who is always honest and never afraid to speak her mind in the interest I do well. Her opinion matters.

To Keidi my publisher who saw something in my writing and who today calls me a prolific poet. Thank you for everything.

Finally, my parents who have gone on their journey home, which I call next door. They have given me these gifts and have always taught me to believe in myself. They have embedded values in me that have made me rich in my heart. Their spirit continues to surround me daily and I hope even on a dark day I'll always search out the light.

"The very best poetry has the power to connect to
people, and even touch souls. Tracy Connolly's work
belongs in that category. These poems will make you
think, reflect, and perhaps even change your attitude
and approach to aspects of your life. Enjoy!"

John Dolan
The Echo

Contents

A Birthday Message To Heaven

Today I think of you here with me,
Celebrating your birthday for all to see.
Another year we are apart,
But I hold you here within my heart.

My father, my friend, a teacher to all.
A man who was there, awaiting your call.
A man who put others before his own needs.
A kind-hearted soul who always would please.

There are things I remember as a small child,
Carried around proudly by your side.
You'd rattle your change to let me know,
I'm never without and you'll never let go.

So, your spirit lives on around me today.
A message I'm sending just to say.
Happy Birthday in heaven and all you surround.
As you shine like an angel, beautifully crowned.

Morning Prayer

May all your woes be few
Your heartache fade away
As you enter a new morning
May the light lead the way.

www.tracyconnollyspoetrys.com
@poetsbelief

New Year 2023

As we open up another year,
We long for all around to care,
The homeless sick and dying ones,
Give them the strength to carry on.

Look around when you wake up.
There are endless possibilities you can touch.
New moments, new ideas, adventures to come.
In search for the truth, you've only begun.

As we march past the darkened fear,
Find courage within, let God be near.
Give some light to those who lag behind,
While being encouraging and always kind.

Leave your history behind the curtain,
If reopened, you must be certain.
Have no regrets in your past.
Love your life and make it last.

Be mystified by the beauty of life.
There's unmeasurable learning always in sight.
Take a chance for you may achieve,
Something wonderful, you must believe.

Looking forward, there's lots to do.
Finding new hobbies that match only you.
Living your life, the best that you can.
Fulfilling your dreams and all your plans.

Taking a moment to reflect on who's past,
Knowing one day our moment won't last.
Enjoying the spirits that surround you today,
Being thankful to God for one more day.

Love and rejoice, sing and pray,
Dance through this life to feel okay.
The moments like these will make you smile,
Look into your soul and become alive.

Gaze at the world bringing new light,
While enjoying the moments that feel right.
Celebrate the crossover to a brand new year,
Be happy in life that you made it here.

If you put love in
what you do
it will grow
its own beauty
©TracyConnolly
20/04/21
poetsbelief

All Soul's Day

The Communion of saints is here.
From the pilgrims on this earth,
The dead who are being purified,
The blessed in heaven's new birth.

Look at temporal goods as borrowed,
For death will soon deprive all.
Lead always with the truth amongst,
And be ready for the ultimate call.

In the creed we profess "I Believe."
In the Communion of saints as one,
As we are all one big family.
Surrounded by the stars, moon, and sun.

Death does not separate us.
It binds us into one church.
Those who go to be purified,
The eternal salvation they search.

All will make it to heaven,
Some will be in God's waiting room.
Let's pray for those gone before us,
Hope that they'll get there soon.

Both heaven and earth are praying,
For the lives and souls needing prayer.
Go and celebrate this holy month,
By kneeling and showing you care.

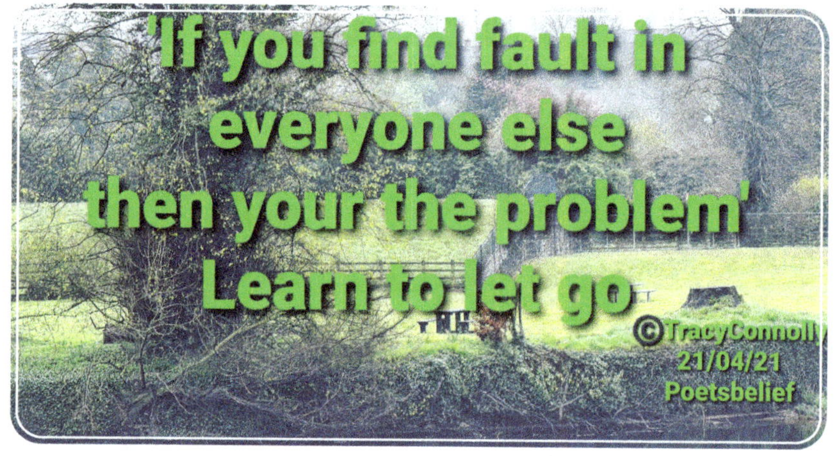
'If you find fault in
everyone else
then your the problem'
Learn to let go
©TracyConnolly
21/04/21
Poetsbelief

**A Poem Written By
Veteran Tracy Connolly,**

An Irish Hero

Ireland has lost a Soldier,
One that was brave and kind.
A Peacekeeper who did his duty,
Never leaving anyone behind.

Private Rooney protected his country,
With pride he raised the Irish flag.
Served with the United Nations on missions,
Soldiering, he was more than glad.

His sacrifices will be remembered,
For the challenges he had to face,
Protecting the vulnerable he surrounded,
Making sure everyone was safe.

Then came that fatal day,
When darkness filled his eyes.
He finished his last duty,
Crossed over into the skies.

I'm sure his father was waiting,
To salute his comrade in arms.
Parading with his army of angels,
His protectors amongst the stars.

Left behind there's a blanket of mourning,
From every corner of the emerald Isle.
We have lost a valiant Soldier,
One of the finest selfless kinds.

You're coming home an Irish hero.
Sadly, we will lay to rest.
Drape you in the tricolour,
Treat you as one of our best.

Sleep easy now, great Soldier.
All that is done, is done.
Be proud you were that Soldier.
You'll be forever Irelands son.

Your passion flows within the realm of
your beauty
So let it flow as your beauty will
expand
TracyConnolly
27/04/21
@Poetsbelief

Be Present

We live in this life,
We hope it goes right,
We dance in the rain,
While forgetting our pain.

No man or no woman,
Should forget who they are.
They must live in the moment,
And believe they'll go far.

Life can be a mystery,
For all that are living.
Let's create the fine moments,
And never stop giving.

Believe in the sun,
The moon and the stars,
For they bring you brightness,
As we move through the dark.

Be present on this journey,
For you'll get only one.
Look towards the light,
Look up to the sun.

Never give up on hope,
That's all we have.
Be surrounded by good energies,
They won't make you sad.

Time is ticking by,
Faster than you know.
Don't spend another moment,
Letting any second go.

People can make you sad,
As they carry their grim pain.
Disrespecting all the good in you,
While creating their own game.

A lesson must be learned,
To believe in who you are.
You're the creator of your destiny,
So, rise and you'll go far.

Remember one more thing,
Be thankful that you're here.
The power is in the moment.
There's always someone who cares.

If your dreams lie stagnant
Deep within your soul
Go and waken them alive
and start to create your goals
© TracyConnolly05/05/21
@poetsbelief

Beyond The Grave

If I fall asleep tonight,
Be happy that I'm gone.
Life for me is over.
I'm up where I belong.

My journey was all good,
I'm happy to report.
Life has been a gift.
No one should sell it short.

I certainly have no regrets.
I lived with a conscience clear.
Always helping the misfortunate,
And ones that I hold dear.

If my life was to play again,
I'd leave it like before.
Being grateful for my being,
And a life that I adored.

Thinking about the problems,
I'd ask you to think again.
This life is very precious.
One day it soon will end.

Be mindful who you meet,
Not everyone is the same.
Forgive them for their flaws,
And never be ashamed.

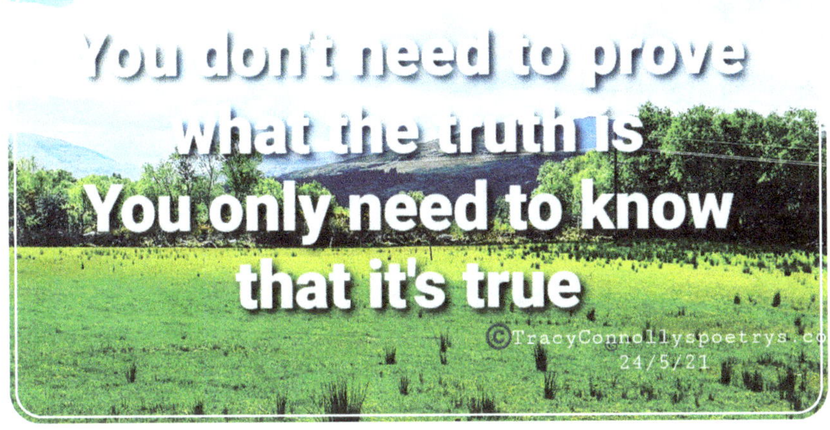
You don't need to prove
what the truth is
You only need to know
that it's true
©TracyConnollyspoetrys.co
24/5/21

Country Gardens

A Veteran came to me today,
Requesting a new poem.
I smiled at him for a moment.
If only I had known.

Country Gardens, he did say,
Those gardens they do grow,
And like this veteran centre,
Friends are all we know.

It was magical to see,
The spirit within his eyes.
He felt at home amongst others,
He belonged just for awhile.

It's not the garden in his head,
Although it's special to suggest,
It's really the comradery,
And getting stuff off his chest.

But as I turned to the door,
I could see the colours bright,
Propping up their heads abloom,
Multicolours giving us delight.

I continued out the door,
Admiring from the lawn.
The polytunnel standing firm.
All at work, I was drawn.

I entered a new garden,
One that was taking flight.
All the bulbs that were planted,
Flourished and now in sight.

For a moment I was taken,
By the growth that was within.
Everything was sprouting fast,
Where do I begin?

Plucking out the onions,
Holding them in my hands.
Never did I imagine,
This beauty at a glance.

Surrounded by many greens.
Being proud to see its flourish.
It took many strong hands to create.
A presence always to encourage.

This garden is in the city,
With a country garden feel.
Like a majestic outdoor arena,
And an audience to its appeal.

There's time in life to pause.
It might not be your time.
But always make time for others,
Even when asked just for a rhyme.

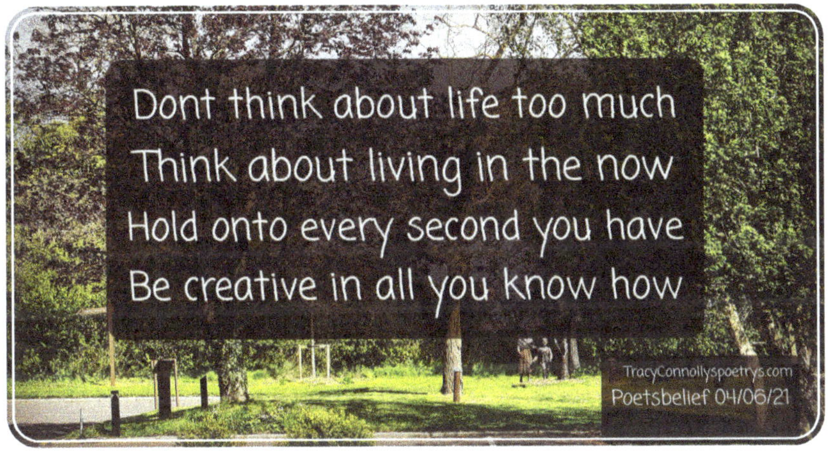
Dont think about life too much
Think about living in the now
Hold onto every second you have
Be creative in all you know how
TracyConnollyspoetrys.com
Poetsbelief 04/06/21

Daddy

The silent sound,
You're not around.
Hurts my heart,
You did part.

On that day,
You went away.
I cried then,
For you to stay.

A broken heart.
Tears did fall.
There's no recovery,
From it all.

You are gone,
To a mighty place,
For I myself,
Too will face.

It's not easy,
To let go.
Your spirit lingers,
This I know.

I must try,
To carry on.
Put my words,
Within a song.

The words will be;
I love you so.
The day you left,
I pleaded no.

Sometimes in life,
You are surprised,
About the departure,
To the skies.

I tell myself,
We'll meet again.
Our love was strong,
It knows no end.

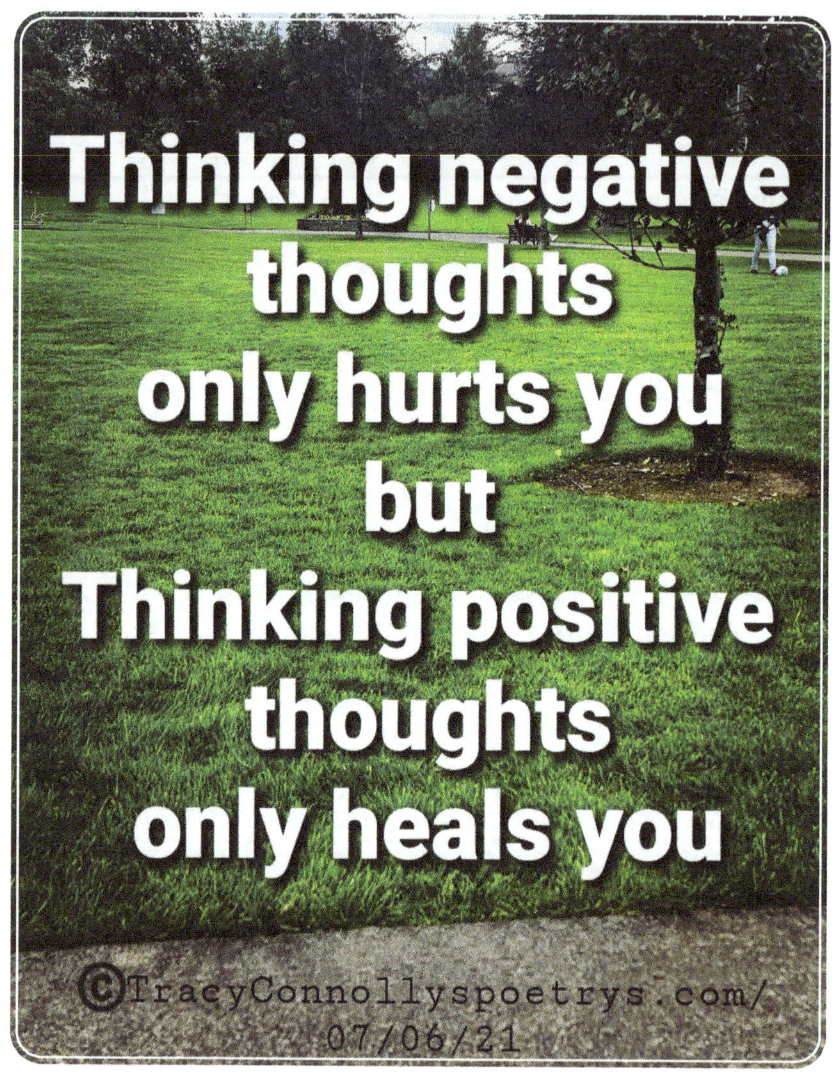
Thinking negative
thoughts
only hurts you
but
Thinking positive
thoughts
only heals you
©TracyConnollyspoetrys.com/
07/06/21

Eighteen Years Later

From the moment I held you,
You put sparkle in my life.
Gripping my hand tightly.
I was smitten in your eyes.

As the years did unfold,
You became my amazing girl.
Bringing joy to my heart,
And adding greatness to my world.

Then came the teenage years,
Where tears began to flow.
You relied upon my advice,
Only a mother could know.

Your independence and strength grew,
As you climbed the workforce chain.
All the while attending college,
And mastering fitness as your aim.

You continue to impress me,
With your never-ending drive,
In your life, your ambitious,
And your focus is your guide.

You're my one and only daughter.
You're of a special kind.
One that I was granted.
And never again will find.

You're stunning and I love you.
You're kind to all I know.
You have that certain aura,
In any room you'll glow.

Today is your big birthday,
Only once you'll turn eighteen.
You've fledged into a woman.
You're looking towards your dreams.

My closing message is easy,
Take pride in who you are.
Celebrate your birthday,
And shine just like a star.

Live life as if a
Miracle
Happened
©Tracyconnollyspoetrys.co
@poetsbelief
14/06/21

Every Minute Counts

It struck a chord with me,
As you sat upon your chair.
You looked solemn in your moment.
There was a chill within the air.

I looked at you so sadly,
Your life had passed on by.
You were trying to make conversation,
There was tears within your eyes.

You expressed moments of happiness,
Just because I was there,
You brought back flooding memories,
Long ago and now you cared.

It's difficult and so upsetting,
Now your old and frail.
A heart so full of love.
Precious moments that we inhale.

Now you're seeing life differently,
You know what it's all about.
You take pleasure in each moment,
And make every minute count.

When it's time to say goodbye,
There's a sadness upon your face,
But you brush it off so quickly,
It's your smile that I embrace.

Our lives go by real fast,
We must cherish life each day.
And try to find some joy,
To make us feel okay.

Never think your day is over,
As the moments are alive.
They remind us of the beauty,
And it's promise to survive.

So, when you're feeling lonely,
And you need someone to call,
I'll be there in the background,
I'll be there when you fall.

Time is all we have,
We must enjoy it while we can,
And be there for one another.
As God only knows its plan.

Try to surround yourself with people who understand your beautiful soul Instead of you trying hard for them not to kill your spirit...

@poetsbelief
06/01/23 ©

Here Once More

They say that times a healer.
I'm not too sure about that.
For when you left this earth,
All I wanted was you back.

No one knows the pain I carry,
As I hide my tears away.
You were the greatest father.
I miss you more each day.

There's a Robin in my garden,
He visits from time to time.
I call him by your name,
He sings just like a rhyme.

Today would have been your birthday,
I'd have been right by your side,
Told you that I loved you,
You'd return it with a smile.

Life is what we make it,
I know this now for sure.
It doesn't get any easier.
I wish you were here once more.

I feel your presence near me,
As I write this poem for you.
A connection that won't be broken,
We were a special kind of two.

I promise I'll never forget you,
I'll keep you in my heart.
I love you and I miss you,
We'll never be apart.

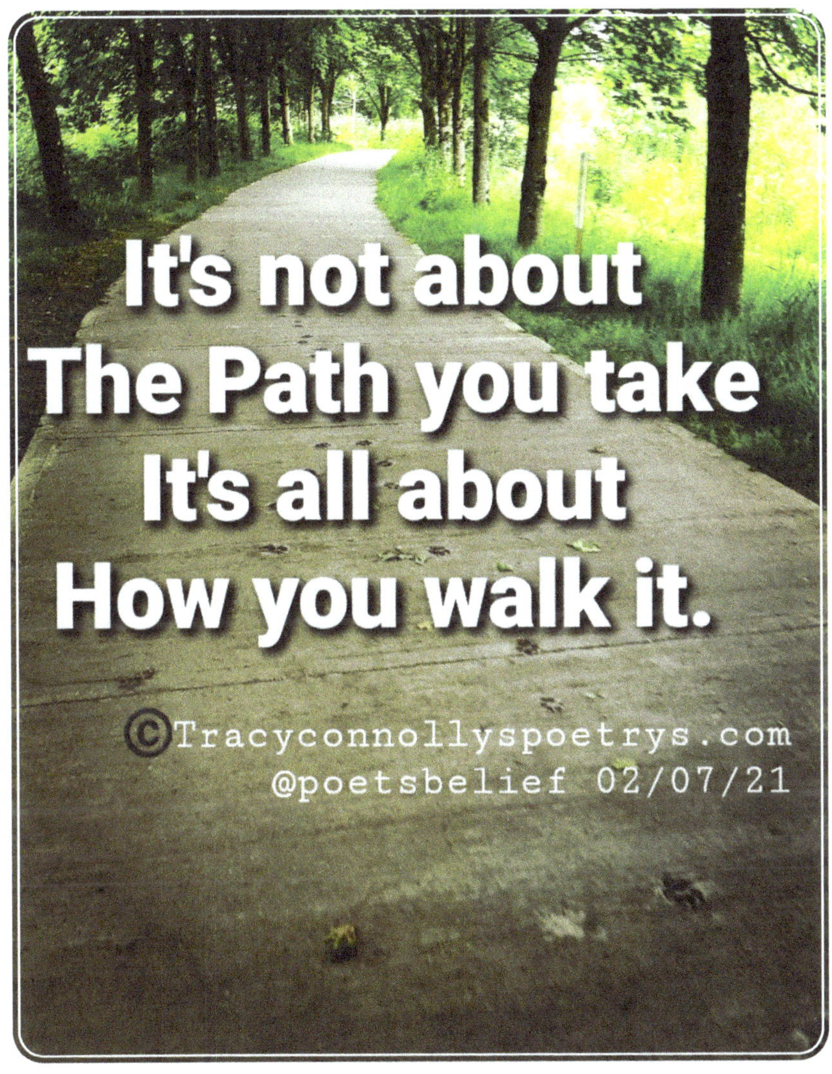
It's not about
The Path you take
It's all about
How you walk it.
©Tracyconnollyspoetrys.com
@poetsbelief 02/07/21

Hero Of Many

A boy is all he was,
Back in 1961.
A battlefield he would meet.
Life's circus soon begun.

His name was Matt Quinlan.
One of many to survive,
The horrors of the Congo,
The fight to stay alive.

He led a mortar crew,
Where Irish roots did show.
A tactical-minded young soldier,
A defence for every blow.

Fighting from a mortorpit,
With no camouflage to display.
A genius for grid-referencing,
A target for gunplay.

His courage was heroic,
As he took the enemy down.
Shelling targets from a distance,
The battlefield was his ground.

Then a ceasefire was announced,
The battle came to a halt.
He celebrated his victory,
By giving up the assault.

The time thereafter wasn't nice,
Being held captive night after night,
Negotiations happened and all were released.
Homeward bound and mission complete.

Being home on Irish soil,
Wasn't meant to be.
So, he packed his bags quickly,
To Winton, he did flee.

His story is only one,
Of many who were erased,
From the Hall of Heroes.
And the service that they gave.

Now you are in God's home.
Your duties are all done.
Be proud of being that soldier,
For you're one of Ireland's sons.

Sometimes in life you have
to let go of what's not for
you and hold on to what's
for you
©Tracyconnollyspoetrys.com
@poetsbelief07/07/21

Homelessness Fear

I've looked on lives throughout my years.
I've seen the pain, I've seen the tears.
The cold shed blood, you were alone.
A darkened alley with no home.

The cries and moans just went unheard.
A shattered life now so blurred.
The loss was great a family torn.
The reflective memories now you scorn.

Your walk feels long on one's own,
Like the devil's crossing a point unknown.
The fight goes on you plead your way,
To see the light and see the day.

You're not sure how this did become.
You're here now and the sun is gone.
You pray to God to save your soul,
And one last chance he may unfold.

The cobbled stone you always see,
As you walk around the streets hungry.
A head hung low, a path not right.
You're sinking fast but you must fight.

You hear the laughter from another's mouth.
You feel so shameful, you're still in doubt,
That you are here and they are well.
You long for happiness, I can tell.

You're tired now so you pick a spot,
To rest your bones, to calm this rot.
You sit in thought they pass you by,
You'd hope they'd stop just for awhile.

You know you're sorry it got this far,
But one did stumble out too far.
Your beating heart throbs in pain,
If only life was back again.

So, let's not judge on what we see.
Our Lord fell three times to his knees.
Let's look upon this as a call,
For our humanity to conquer all.

Lifes joyful mystery
Flourishes into what
Can be
And the beauty that
Surrounds us will be
Forever adored.
©Tracyconnollyspoetrys.com
@poetsbelief 20/07/21

Imagination of Thoughts

Tree branches, moving leaves that cling on.
Crows loud and cackling in flight.
Trickling of rain against the window ledge.
Damp trodden grass, mucky and stained.

Loud wind pushing open the back gate.
Hurling the sound, still of wintertime.
Pockets of uneven ground dampen the view.
A shaken fence that's old but still stands.

Sitting in silence as if I were blind,
Listening deeply as too many birds surround,
Making different noises as some travel far,
Looking for food beneath the bramble filled lawn.

Tired body aches while holding one's head.
Aware of the breath in the present time.
Light heart pondering upon thoughts past.
Weeping memories of faded scenes once were.

Time that's pressured into future happenings.
Unknown pictures taking place as we dream.
Love thy neighbour as the walls are thin.
Be resilient in storms of local gossip.

Finding one's faith on holy days array.
Promises made to future chaplains in prayer.
Adventures being sought in one's promise to self.
Kind-hearted spirit trusting the force of now.

tracyconnollyspoetrys.com
Beauty is not just
within us
Beauty surrounds us
too.

Katie Taylor

There's no defeat for Katie,
She's a winner in her mind.
She sacrificed every moment.
Women's boxing is alive.

She's our world champion,
Until she says she's done.
If she wants a rematch,
Let the fight be run.

Her faith will get her through this,
As she knows it's not the end.
She's a fighter for her country,
It's this we should commend.

She's worked hard in her game.
She's the best that she can be.
She's loved by all of Ireland,
And that's incredible to see.

Just a message for you, Katie,
"You're a champion in our eyes.
The forever Bray bomber,
And we're thankful you're alive."

Either you drown in the ocean of
existence
Or be powerful in the presence of the
now
©Tracyconnollyspoetrys.com
@poetsbelief 27/07/21

Lessons In Life

I look at my life right now,
It's important to see where I'm going.
The journey is all I have,
And I must keep on moving.

As a child, I had no fear.
I played with all my toys.
My parents were always there for me,
And my dog was forever loyal.

When I became of teenage years,
I joined many a musical band.
It brought light within my soul,
And never did that feeling end.

I never really thought of time.
I guess life was really full.
I was chasing dreams I wanted.
My mind would not sit still.

Today I look upon my life,
A life I know I lived.
Took many chances with no regrets.
I still have more to give.

This is my time to flourish.
I have learnt lessons in life,
Where ignorance was acceptable,
In awful scenes that were rife.

I'm living for today,
Tomorrow may never come.
This moment is all I have,
I'm nowhere near to being done.

When you find yourself
At your
Pivotal of happiness
Don't try to explain
Just feel gratitude
For its presence

www.tracyconnollyspoetrys.com
@poetsbelief

Live As You Know How

What inspires you?
What takes you on your course?
What enlightens you?
What's giving you the source?

The days you wake,
Are days you should be glad.
You woke to see another day,
And remember what you have.

If you dream a dream,
Don't close it in a box.
Find a way to follow through,
And see where it unlocks.

Be mindful of the potholes,
You'll fall in one or two.
Never let that bother you,
As you'll rise again anew.

Someday you'll see the darkness,
Other days you'll see the light.
But no matter where you stand,
Count on life being bright.

I'll leave you with this thought,
Enjoy your life for now.
Time cannot be taken back.
Go live as you know how.

Knowing what you have
already
Is better than not
knowing what you want

www.tracyconnollyspoetrys.com
©16/10/22

Memories Live On

Whenever I think of you,
I know you are at peace.
I feel your spirit near me,
In my soul to keep.
I can't say that it's easy,
To think of you as gone.
My father and my mother,
It's you who made me strong.
I love you and I miss you,
Each day that does unfold.
Where memories live on,
Until I'm grey and old.

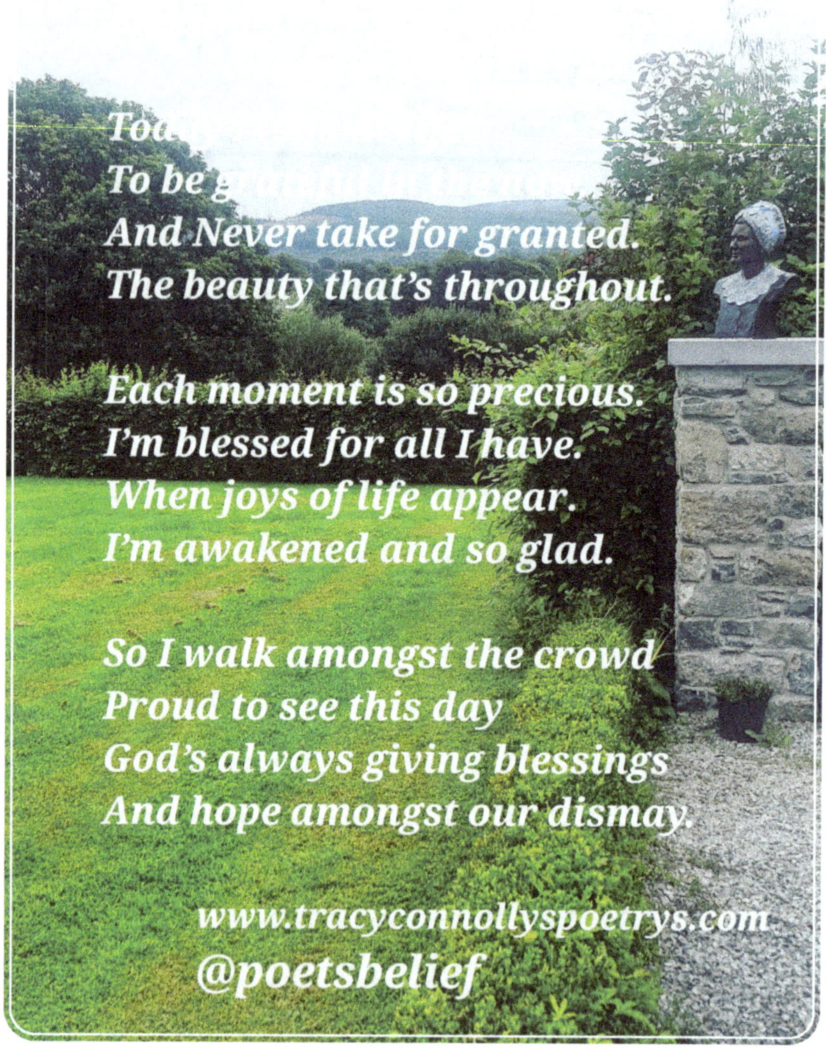
Toa
To be g
And Never take for granted.
The beauty that's throughout.

Each moment is so precious.
I'm blessed for all I have.
When joys of life appear.
I'm awakened and so glad.

So I walk amongst the crowd
Proud to see this day
God's always giving blessings
And hope amongst our dismay.

www.tracyconnollyspoetrys.com
@poetsbelief

Message In A Bottle

When I was just a child,
I swam beneath the sea,
Hoping that I'd come ashore,
And find a note for me.

Later in my teenage years,
I'd swim the sea once more.
Craving that I'd see a sign,
Outspread on the sandy floor.

At nighttime I would dream,
Of better days to come.
Dreaming of a big surprise,
That life would soon be fun.

Standing barefoot on the sand,
I'd look out to the sea,
Hoping that one sunny day,
You'd come and marry me.

I was looking for that object,
The one that holds the key.
There I'd find deep within,
Floating here to me.

I questioned its delay,
As the days were long.
For something that was small,
In my heart, it did belong.

Those days I do remember,
Longing for the truth.
Looking at the stars above,
Eager in my youth.

What was it all for?
And why did I not see?
The message in the bottle,
Had presented it to me.

I rushed to catch the bottle,
I wanted far too long.
I held it in my hand,
It made me feel strong.

I looked around and knew,
The years had passed on by,
I didn't need that bottle,
You were standing by my side.

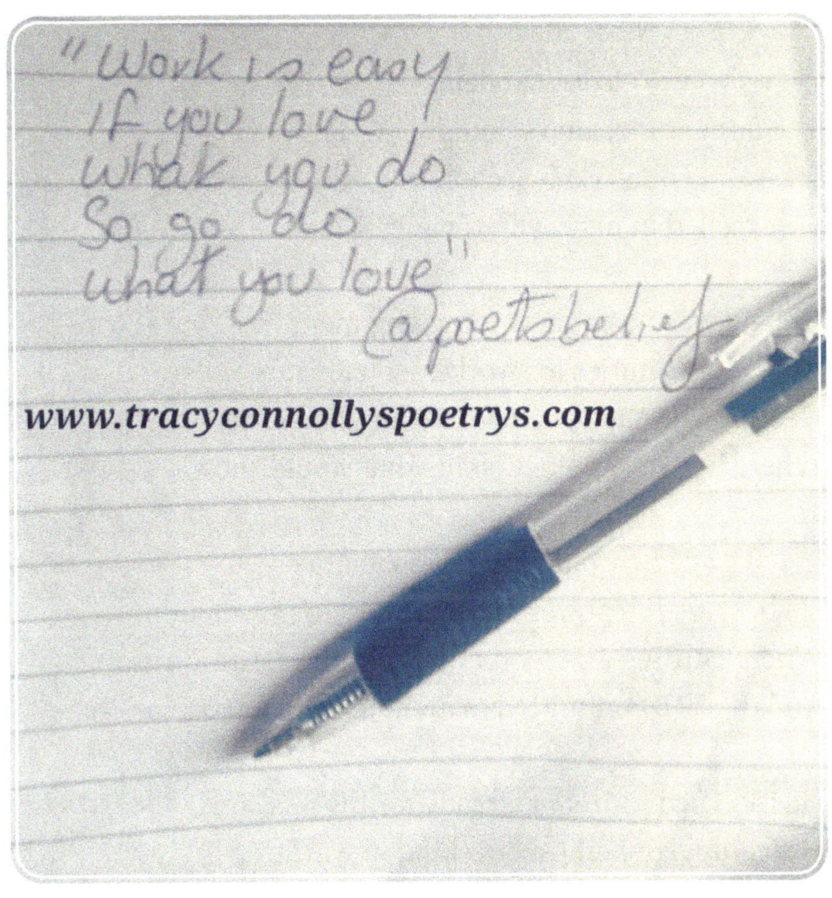
"Work is easy
if you love
what you do
So go do
what you love"
@poetsbelief
www.tracyconnollyspoetrys.com

Michael Collins (The Big Fellow)

He was our Nelson Mandela,
The father of Ireland's Sons.
He was a young rising scholar,
He excelled in his native tongue.

Ireland was no country for young men,
And opportunities for workers fell low.
He sailed on the seas to London,
Where he acquired new skills that would show.

In a decade he would show great stance.
He became the powerhouse of Ireland's revolution,
Where Hurling and football became a recruiting ground,
And the IRB committed to an independent conclusion.

He returned to Ireland, ready for his mission.
His campaign being a new kind of warfare.
He was ruthless but efficient,
He was the most wanted man in the empire.

Collins made it his sworn mission,
That he would achieve an Irish Republic.
Putting the people of Ireland at the forefront.
As if a prophesied democratic.

He never knew when he was beaten,
He always learnt from his mistakes.
Everything for him was a learning experience.
Sinn Fein's University he'd embrace.

He established an intelligent network,
Like a blanket that covered Eire's land.
Locating safe houses and appointing messengers,
He was a man more than grand.

Welfare funds for Veterans and widows,
Were some of the tasks he held close.
Giving key positions to volunteers, IRB, Sinn Féin,
A rising Irish star in that you'd take note.

He showed bravery, he showed leadership.
He was a genius throughout his life.
He was the man you'd look up to,
And he wasn't afraid to fight.

A Soldier, a statesman, a diplomat,
An intellect who was more than great.
With only one burning ambition,
To free this country and state.

Your biggest
challenge
in life is being you

@poetsbelief

'MISSY'

How do I get the words out?
What more is there to say?
You were given wings to fly,
I'm here, left alone to stay.

I remember when you were small,
Your smile would light up a room.
Grandad Michael would be your hero,
You were stuck together like glue.

You wanted to join the army,
As you became independently strong.
Your nature and charisma was shining,
You helped everybody along.

You had a gorgeous, generous nature.
One that I'll never forget.
Kindhearted words for everyone,
Shared with all that you met.

Such a beautiful and vibrant young woman,
God had a plan for you.
He picked you from this earth,
An angel he knew was true.

Where do I go from here?
What do I say to you all?
I'll never recover from this moment,
I'll always remember the call.

As a father, I'm broken hearted.
You will always be daddy's girl.
I'll never let go of my 'Missy.'
You'll be forever there in my world.

Dont take this life for granted
Today is all you've got
Put pleasure in the moment
Be thankful that's your lot

www.tracyconnollyspoetrys.com
@poetsbelief

Moral Injury

Who are we to judge our own,
Who travelled abroad to the horrors unknown?
Who are we to look down on them,
When they served their country as great men?

Who are we to forget their pain,
When they battled together on the Congo's plain?
Who are we to say no to them,
For they've earned their medal or even ten?

Who are we when we see men fade,
To a shadow of themselves in this charade?
Who are we when we let them down,
When they called for help on Ireland's ground?

Who are we when they were left behind,
For their forgotten braveries to help mankind?
Who are we to hush their voice,
As they try to speak and avoid the noise?

Who are we to avoid their suffering,
After much bloodshed and years of troubling?
Who are we to see a unit thrown,
On Jadotville soil with an outcome unknown?

Who are we to ignore their honour,
Like dismissing results from great scholars?
Who are we to avoid what's true,
But finally give justice to their rescue?

Who are we that causes moral injury,
For it to go down in wrongful history?
Who are we to neglect the signs of loneliness,
Suicides, mental disorders, and unhappiness?

Who are we as an Irish free state?
Known for our sacrifices were never too late.
Who are we to not praise Ireland's sons,
As they battle together for justice being done?

Love the things you do
Create your own happiness
We come into the world alone
And we leave the world alone
You are your own strength
Learn to recognise it

www.tracyconnollyspoetrys.com
@poetsbelief

Mother's First Anniversary

The day God took you home,
Left a scar within my heart.
The feeling of emptiness filled me,
My world was torn apart.

It's been one year since you've passed.
Those feelings pierce me once again.
Now all I have is memories,
Of life we lived back then.

I remember where you used to sit,
The songs you used to sing.
Those were our happiest moments.
The joy that it would bring.

It's sad to think you're not home.
When I call, you're not there.
The silence is deafening to my ears.
I look down and shed a tear.

I hope you found that inner peace,
Far beyond amongst the stars.
Please know that you are loved,
And forever in my heart.

Success is not just
Good luck.
Success is hard work
And dedication.
A fire within your soul.
A flame you cannot
Quench.
www.tracyconnollyspoetrys.
com

My Best Friend

Poetry is what saved me,
Amongst the fire within my soul.
Nothing was going to break me,
Along my tired little road.

It gave peace amid the rain,
That poured from the heavens above.
And even when it dried up,
It still became my love.

Poetry is my best friend.
I love it more and more.
It appears in its true form,
When it wants to be explored.

When I retire for the night,
Poetry stays on my mind.
When I rise within the morning,
I'm blessed the poetry comes alive.

If the choice arose tomorrow,
To leave poetry shelved away,
A part of me would wither,
And would slowly see decay.

What I know for sure,
Is to cease the moment now.
Keep growing with the poetry,
And I'll never see a cloud.

Even when it rains in life
A rainbow will follow after
No matter what the storm
Your life is all that matters
www.tracyconnollyspoetrys.com
@poetsbelief

My Mother

Today is Mother's day,
And I'm without my mother.
I know she's shining down.
If only I could hug her.

The feeling is so raw,
As her presence is just gone.
Oh, I miss my mother.
This day, it feels so wrong.

I passed the shopping aisle,
Where cards were on display,
They read "Happy Mother's Day."
The pain doesn't go away.

I know I should be happy,
As we celebrate Mother's day.
But God took my mother.
Another angel come to stay.

As I look back on life,
I'm thankful for all she did.
There was no greater mother.
Every promise she did fill.

So, when you're with your mother,
Think of me today.
For I'm without my mother.
God's angel gone away.

Don't be sad for me.
Just hear my message through.
God has granted you another day.
How lucky to be you.

Celebrate this day with joy.
Hold your mother's hand.
Tell her that you love her.
Let your love expand.

Life doesn't always go to plan.
That's why I say to you,
Go celebrate your Mother's day.
Spread love in all you do.

Time is ticking
Life is short
make your moments
In your thoughts
www.tracyconnollyspoetrys.com
@poetsbelief

Queen Elizabeth II

A Queen who was a leader,
The mother of all who came.
She held the throne upon her,
She was the monarch's frame.

She reigned her life devoted.
A guide who claimed your soul.
To do good in your lifetime,
And always fulfill your role.

She made her mark to all.
Her devotion was so true.
Her decisions were all final,
A Queen that always knew.

"Her majesty, we will remember,"
I hear the people say.
A reflection we are holding.
Your memory will always stay.

Your leadership and kindness,
Will always throughout remain.
Your dedication for the people,
In their hearts will never change.

They'll miss your warming smile.
Your wave they always knew.
The grandmother of their time.
A person always true.

I know you're shining down.
You want them all to know,
You're in a better place,
A place you are at home.

The King must now take charge,
Your duties are all done.
The people must respect,
Your leader is your son.

You've fallen asleep so calm.
Your spirit still remains.
Now you are in God's land.
Your legacy it must reign.

"I declare before you all,
That my whole life,
Whether it be long or short,
Shall be devoted to your service."

Remember your roots and your army
boots
When times get tough don't give up
There's many battles you once fought
So fight the fight within your
thoughts.

www.tracyconnollyspoetrys.com
@poetsbelief

Remember Me

If I should pass this world today,
Don't be sad because I'm gone.
Think about my life as lived.
I'm up where I belong.

I've lived a life that was complete,
I'm grateful for all I've had,
Now I take away sweet memories.
In my next life, I won't be sad.

Time goes by way too fast.
I never knew this until now.
I've been blessed with all I know.
Support and kindness still surrounds.

Remember me when I'm gone.
Come visit me at my grave.
I'll be there looking down,
From the heavens pearly gates.

I know the end is drawing near.
The Lord beckons me from afar.
I still hope for one more day,
But I'll leave the door ajar.

When someone sends flowers
Their soul shines from afar
Their thoughtful and kind actions
Will be forever in our hearts.

@poetsbelief

Saint Patrick

Being made a slave as a teenager,
Saint Patrick's work had only just begun.
God began to ignite something special.
And he knew this boy was the one.

Every day in Ireland, Patrick tended the sheep.
He prayed every hour he could,
This is where his faith was strengthened,
And his spirit fervent for all he stood.

While lying sleeping, his mind did dream.
God spoke to him, "your ship is ready."
He set off leaving behind his master.
His fears removed while spreading love thereafter.

Its New Year's Day
And I'm glad I called.
I ask for your presense.
To watch over us all.
I pray to you now.
To always be close.
Help a dear loved one.
Each day that unfolds.
The beauty with prayer.
I know your around.
I feel your strong spirit.
With its heavenly surround.
You were a great father.
I could always approach.
The love that you shared.
A heart that just knows.
So goodbye for awhile.
I'll call in again.
Shine light down upon us.
In our heart's you remain.

Say A Prayer

For all the people who are sick.
Persevere as it will be quick.
Find the strength to cope with pain.
As you will see the light again.

It's just a hiccup along the way.
You've got this far, it will be okay.
Say a prayer that you've woken up.
And tell yourself that it's pure luck.

A miracle happened for you today.
So, push those clouds far away.
Think of sunshine from the sky.
It's shining bright for just your eyes.

Look at what you fear the most.
By helping others on their road.
Plant a seed for it to grow,
And spread the word to not let go.

Sometimes in life you flip a coin.
Which doesn't match to bring you joy.
God is telling you he is near,
Live your life because he cares.

So, take a moment to breathe in the air.
See the beauty in all you share.
Life's great mystery has brought you here.
So, live your life without great fear.

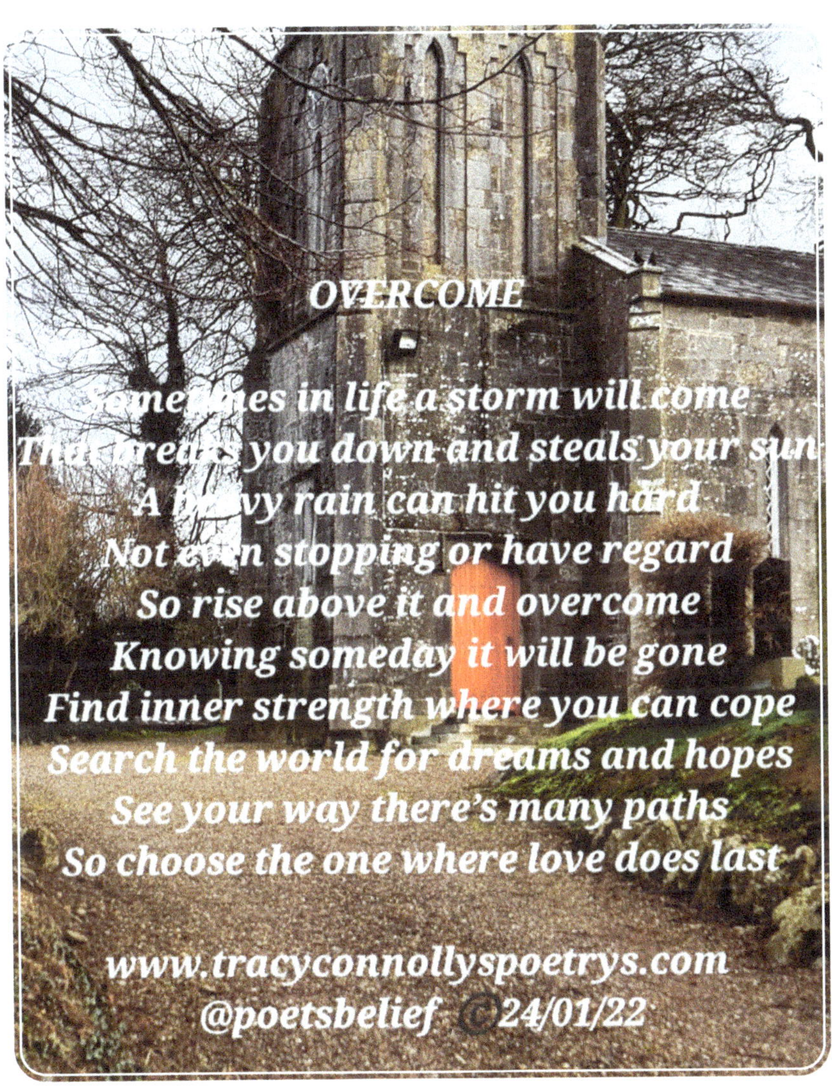

OVERCOME

Sometimes in life a storm will come
That breaks you down and steals your sun
A heavy rain can hit you hard
Not even stopping or have regard
So rise above it and overcome
Knowing someday it will be gone
Find inner strength where you can cope
Search the world for dreams and hopes
See your way there's many paths
So choose the one where love does last

www.tracyconnollyspoetrys.com
@poetsbelief 24/01/22

St. Brigid's Day - Lá Fhéile Bríde

In our beautiful Isle so fair,
Brigid's name echoes through the land.
The daughter of a pagan chief,
Who, like wildfire, God did send.

She was the goddess of healers,
Poets, childbirth, and inspiration.
A goddess of fire, patron of warfare.
And a Saint of many creations.

A life-giving goddess she was known,
As the birth of new lambs appeared,
A joyful spring where flowers bloomed,
And sunshine was finally here.

She comforted her country's poor,
With the gift she did possess.
Leaving behind a sacred legacy.
Saint Brigid of Ireland she was blessed.

Brigid's Cross hangs over the doorway.
We believe God's blessings too.
For anyone who lays eyes on it,
The Lord will shine down on you.

St Brigid's Day

Please bless the cloth I hung today

Give strength and hope in all I say.

Please bless the house I walk within

And free the walls from any sin.

Please shine your light upon my door

A joyous spring here to explore.

Please now surround us from above

Saint Brigid's day we do but love.

www.tracyconnollyspoetrys.com
@poetsbelief 01/02/22

See The Light

Life's a journey we're all on.
Some days your right, some days your wrong.
But be whatever you're to be,
It's not your fault or can't you see.

Don't go around with negative thoughts.
Think of nice things, don't be distraught.
Buy yourself some fancy clothes,
Try them on and do a pose.

Don't be bitter to another's tongue.
Live in the moment. you are young.
Be realistic in how far you'll go.
There's no disappointment or permanent low.

By watching others, you'll learn from them.
Take deep breaths, it's not the end.
Smiling often will help you through.
Be proud you're here and you love you.

Sometimes in life they'll get you down,
Creating pain to make you frown.
Rise above the world that's grey,
And thank the Lord that you're okay.

See the light that shines on you.
It's a brand-new day to start anew.
You found your faith and forgave,
The only life you could save.

Time is your Bank Account
So make Time for it.
www.tracyconnollyspoetrys.com
@poetsbelief ©

The Resurrection

Jesus knew he had to leave this world.
His father was awaiting his homecoming,
Having loved his own in his world.
He loved them and prayed for their forthcoming.

The evening meal was being prepared,
The devil had already prompted Judas.
By betraying Jesus, he thought he had won.
The Lord above gave power down to his son.

Let the truth sink deep down today.
After all the suffering Jesus had done.
Let forgiveness and peace surround us now,
The resurrection of Jesus Christ, we are one.

Dont focus on the land
Just focus on the sea
For the waters are stiring
A message we cant see.

www.tracyconnollyspoetrys.com
@poetsbelief 08/02/2022

Titanic Submarine

Some days I wake,
And holler, "why?"
The pain you carry.
The tears you cry.

You never thought,
Of the last goodbye.
They were coming back,
Not going to die.

An ocean of coastguards,
Air National guard aircraft,
The sub-Prince on the seas,
Looking for them back.

A CEO and billionaire,
Businessman and son,
Mr. Titanic all boarded.
Here today and then gone.

The search was endless,
To the core,
An ocean-wide,
Right to its floor.

The awful feelings,
You felt then.
The crush, the pain.
Where did it end?

The world was hurt,
By your loss alone.
Telling your families,
You won't be home.

The day that's given,
The chance they took.
They never thought,
It was their last look.

Prayers being said,
For those concerned.
God, give them wings,
They've surely earned.

Everyday is a miracle
If you believe it is
www.tracyconnollyspoetrys.com
@poetsbelief

This Beautiful Life

Take your time.
Life is short.
Don't push too hard.
Don't be distraught.
Think of good things,
That make you see,
This beautiful life,
All that can be.
Remember the moments,
That made you smile.
Think of them fondly,
Even just for awhile.
Life's an adventure,
It's a mystery as well.
Tomorrow is not promised.
Let go and don't dwell.

We may not be in your
country
or feeling your great pain
but we're praying for your
safety
and freedom to come your
way

www.tracyconnollyspoetrys.com
@poetsbelief 28/02/22

Tsunami Of Grief

Devastation struck the community.
Ireland's collective hearts did stop.
Creeslough was full of tragedy,
Everyone went into shock.

Fire services and ambulances personnel,
Went quickly to the scene.
A helicopter floated overhead,
Looking on sights unforeseen.

The serious and multiple injuries,
Required immediate and fast response.
An explosion causing major damage,
Onlookers were in a trance.

As the news continued to ripple,
And the deaths were rising up.
Lord, help the caring hands,
With all the chaos and disrupts.

A village that's now damaged.
They will never forget the day,
When a tsunami of grief hit,
And the county of Donegal became grey.

Some here have gone before us,
Others we'll have to see.
Dear God above, protect them.
Whatever will be, will be.

We must put our hands together,
Be stronger than before.
Pray for all the suffering,
And help everyone ashore.

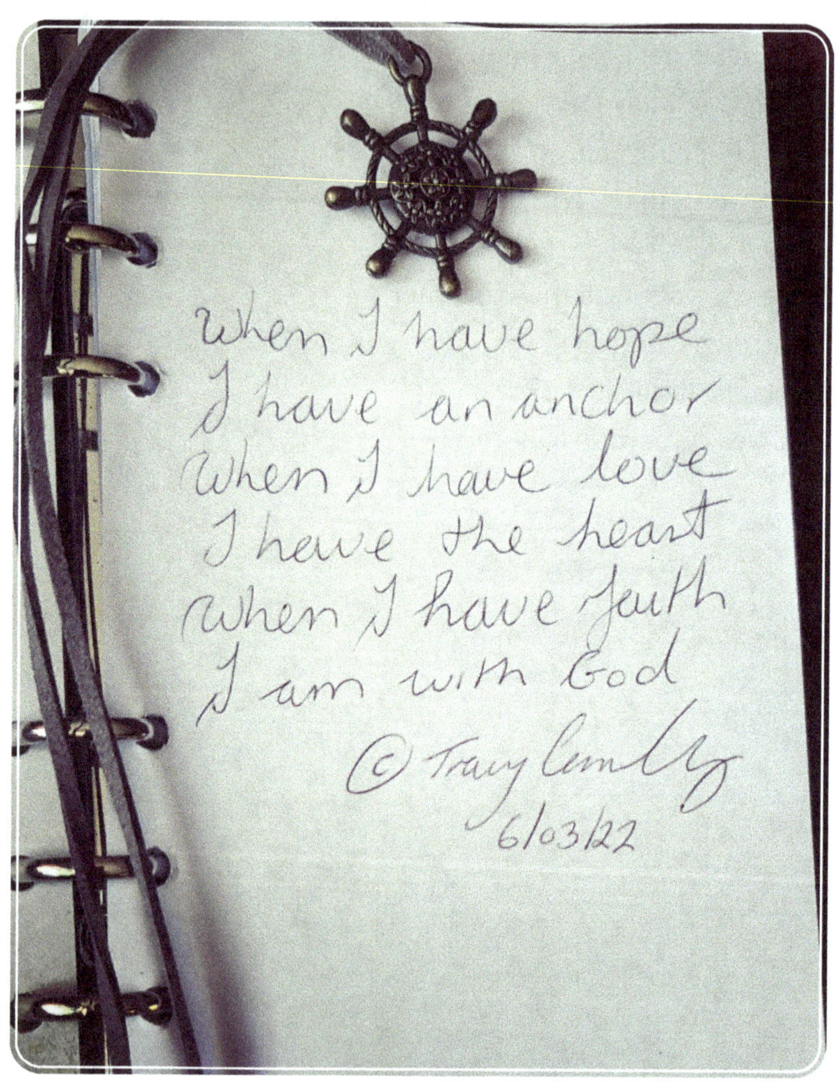
When I have hope
I have an anchor
When I have love
I have the heart
When I have faith
I am with God
© Tracy Connolly
6/03/22

Vicky Phelan Tribute

I heard the news of your passing.
My body went into shock.
Tears came rolling down my cheeks.
A woman that was everyone's rock.

Cervical Cancer Campaigner Vicky Phelan.
You fought the fight for women.
With extraordinary courage, you gave us hope.
Way beyond or expected from any human.

You always spoke about your journey.
Your mission for action, change, accountability.
Those words are now your legacy.
For women there must have changeability.

You struck us with your powerful strength.
Your commitment to the public good.
Not only for the women of Ireland.
But for this country you stood.

Your tireless efforts will not go in vain.
Despite the personal toll you took on.
You protected the lives of women.
You will be honoured after you're gone.

Your record of advocacy was unique.
Your traits of honesty were perpetual.
Your smile and laughter will be eternal,
And in our hearts you'll remain special.

Your endless fight for truth uncovered.
Your justice for all won through.
You fought for us until the end.
Your time had come and you knew.

The world will mourn your soul forever.
For you were one of a kind.
Always caring and thoughtful to others.
You never left anyone behind.

An Angel sits on the throne tonight.
They know they've got a rare find.
For Vicky was one in a million.
I'm sure they're glad she's arrived.

Saint Patrick

As we gather here on St Patricks day.
Across the world a shamrock display.
Song and dance will unearth us all.
Bring us together like old days
recalled.

Lets not forget the reason we come.
Celebrating St Patrick for all he has
done.
Enjoy the love thats given so free.
Go spread the peace to all that you
see.

www.tracyconnollyspoetrys.com
© Tracy Connolly 17/03/22

Who Are We

Who are we to judge our own
Who travelled abroad to the horrors unknown
Who are we to look down on them
When they served their country as great men

Who are we to forget their pain
When they battle together on the Congo's plain
Who are we to say no to them
For they've earned their medal or even ten

Who are we when we see men fade
To a shadow of themselves in this charade
Who are we when we let them down
When they call for help on Irelands ground

Who are we when they were left behind
For their forgotten braveries to help mankind
Who are we to hush their voice
As they try to speak and avoid the noise

Who are we to ignore their sufferings
After much bloodshed and years of troubling
Who are we to see a unit thrown
On Jadotville soil with an outcome unknown

Who are we to ignore their honour
Like dismissing results from great scholars
Who are we to avoid what's true
But finally give justice to their rescue

Who are we that causes moral Injury
For it to go down in wrongful history
Who are we to neglect the signs of loneliness
Suicides, mental disorders and unhappiness

Who are we as an Irish free state
Known for our sacrifices were never too late
Who are we to not praise Irelands sons
As they battle together for justice being done

Live today
Like there's
Never gonna be
Tomorrow
www.tracyconnollyspoetrys.com
@poetsbelief ©

You

When I met you,
I knew it then,
You were my life,
I'd hope to spend.

I crave the moments,
Ever since we met.
Your surprise thrilled me.
My life was set.

You're sexy as hell,
With eyes so brown.
I'll wear the necklace,
You wear the crown.

So, take my hand,
And lead the way.
Kiss me softly.
Don't go away.

Whisper the sounds,
I long to hear.
Gripping me tightly,
Always be near.

When you look at life
See beauty in its face
It's an incredible reminder
To give it honour and much
grace.
www.tracyconnollyspoetrys.com
24/04/22 ©

You're My Valentine

There's something really special,
I love about your way,
Your thoughtfulness and kindness,
Always brightens up my day.

You came into my life.
You swept me off my feet.
With an incredible personality,
One day I hoped I'd meet.

I'm glad we are together,
That it's you and me.
A moment that I cherish.
No place I'd rather be.

There's nothing you can say,
Or try to love me more.
The wonder of your beauty,
The man that I adore.

The years just fly on by,
And we're stronger than before.
I give you all my love.
You give me so much more.

You're my valentine today,
And everyday that comes.
No matter where we are,
You're the light that brings the sun.

Take your time
Feel your gain
Not every day
Will be the same
Let it out
Don't keep it in
Release your thoughts
That are within
Speak your mind
Don't think it through
Just be yourself
Let you be you.

www.tracyconnollyspoetrys.com

You're Not Far Away

If tears were rivers,
Then they'd be a flood.
You're gone forever.
You'll always be loved.

You're not long gone.
You're not far away.
You live in my memory,
Here you will stay.

The gift of life,
You gave to me.
I was really lucky,
That, now I see.

A mother who lived,
Right to the end.
Cared for her children,
And was a godsend.

I'm sending a kiss,
To the heavens above.
May your birthday be great,
And they wrap you in love.

Do things that make you happy
Smile because you are free
Live life as an adventure
Be who you want to be
www.tracyconnollyspoetrys.com

Tracy Connolly's Bio

I was a soldier for 23 years and there are two war heroes on either side of my family. They have been decorated with distinguished service medals from the Congo. Most of my family were in the army. I've been in the war called Operation Grapes of Wrath in 1996 in Lebanon. It's something that will haunt me forever. I've also been to war-torn Kosovo, in 2001. I was proud to be a United Nations Peacekeeper because I love to help others. I'm now a retired Veteran. I work as a tour guide on heritage sites. I do spend a lot of my time focused on my writing and singing. This is where I gravitate to. When I started writing I found a way to help others through my poetry. My first book, *Poetsbelief On Lockdown*, was published in Dec 2020 and my second book, *A Message From Poetsbelief*, was published in 2022. It's exciting to be finally publishing my third book, *Remedies Of Poetry*. I'd like to think with my poetry anything can evolve. I've been published in many newspapers across Ireland in the last few years. Today some of my poems continue to transform into song and I'm working towards my debut album with such a variety of song. I have written and composed all my songs.

I love to write and I love the people who I connect with. The people who follow me are amazing.

You can find some of my poetry and videos on Facebook via this link below:

https://m.facebook.com/poetsbelief/
I'm also on twitter @poetsbelief, Instagram poetsbelief, and youtube Tracy Connolly.